DREAM

&

BELIEVE

—◦⟨⟨❀⟩⟩◦—

The Celestial Art of Creating in Soul Alignment

Anna-Karin Björklund

ARS METAPHYSICA

an imprint of Sunbury Press, Inc.
Mechanicsburg, PA USA

ARS METAPHYSICA

an imprint of Sunbury Press, Inc.
Mechanicsburg, PA USA

FIRST ARS METAPHYSICA EDITION: June 2020

Set in Adobe Garamond | Interior design by Crystal Devine | Cover design by Lawrence Knorr | Edited by Lawrence Knorr.

Publisher's Cataloging-in-Publication Data
Names: Björklund, Anna-Karin, author.
Title: Dream & believe : the celestial art of creating in soul alignment / Anna-Karin Björklund.
Description: First trade paperback edition. | Mechanicsburg, PA : Ars Metaphysica, 2020.
Summary: When you live from the loving frequency of your soul's home, you gracefully flow in harmony with the creative energies of the Universe. This is where you remember your highest purpose and begin to fulfill the dream of your soul.
Identifiers: ISBN: 978-1-620063-74-3 (softcover).
Subjects: BODY, MIND & SPIRIT / Dreams | SELF-HELP / Dreams.

Product of the United States of America
0 1 1 2 3 5 8 13 21 34 55

Continue the Enlightenment!

TO ALL SOUL EXPLORERS,

MAY YOU ALWAYS REACH FOR THE COSMOS,
AND CHERISH THE WONDERS
OF YOUR IMAGINATION

Contents

Introduction

THE GOLDEN KEY to dream fulfillment is found in your imagination. With a devoted practice of imagining good possibilities, you can train yourself to flow in harmony with the loving energies of the Universe—and have fun doing it!

Dream & Believe offers inspiration and guidance for imagining and creating with crystal clarity. Over the chapters ahead, we'll fly in over the golden plane of possibilities—a highly vibrational frequency where you will be invited to co-create your own master blueprint for visualizing and manifesting your dreams. With the help of your imagination, you can elegantly tap into a magnificent field of possibilities whenever you feel like it.

Wherever you choose to be in your imagination does not only hold the key to where you want to be but can also help you realize how you'd really like to *feel*—and as we will soon see, this is one of the key steps to dream fulfillment. When you feel aligned with what you wish for, and become one with this energy source, you reach a state of consciousness where you beautifully attract even more opportunities for living a life in flow.

As with everything in the Universe, this book vibrates with its own frequency. There is a reason you're now holding it in your hands. The moment you picked it up, you signaled to the Universe that you're ready to dream and believe, set clear intentions, and transcend into a loving state of conscious awareness. By engaging in activities that inspire us on a deep soul level, we automatically imagine and visualize how we'd like to feel—and it's when we *believe it* and *feel it*, that things begin to happen.

When you live and dream in love, an abundance of sacred teachings come flowing into your life. Wisdom can be found anywhere and shows up when we are open to receiving it. The book is written as an illuminating guide for those of us who are seeking to live the dream of our soul. Each chapter flows with its own set of sacred ruminations and practices. The intention behind the ruminative reflections and mindful practices is to fill you with golden inspiration for living with an open heart and flowing in the direction of your highest dreams. It is recommended that you take your time to reflect upon the messages in each chapter with your whole heart and soul. The soulful practices will help bring about a vibrational shift in your life.

There is an ocean of loving wisdom within our reach. The sail lifts when we are ready to believe, feel, and align ourselves with what it is we wish for. *Dream & Believe* is filled with ruminative reflections and affirmations for flowing in the direction of your dreams—right from the comfort of wherever you may be. When there is no limitation placed in your mind on what you can achieve, the sky literally is the limit.

Dream and believe, and so it will be.

Anna-Karin Björklund

1

Imagine with Intention

THERE IS AN inner magnificence that reverberates all around when you live and dream in golden alignment with your soul's home. When you remember your soul connection, you become aware of the divine guidance you receive, and beautifully begin to dream beyond illusionary limitations. You dare to dream greatly, set clear intentions, and live with purpose.

Limitless dreaming does not only hold the key to where you want to be, but can also help you realize how you'd like to feel. Identifying how you'd like to feel, and then tuning into this frequency, is a wonderful celestial step on the path of finding alignment with your true soul calling and living a highly vibrational life. When you are aligned with your soul, and become one with this energy vibration, you are in a state of consciousness that attracts even more opportunities for living an elevated life in love and flow. Loving reverberations can be felt in all directions from a soul in high frequency.

> It is in this highly vibrational soul frequency
> that your golden imagination
> gives birth to a clear intention,
> and turns it into creation!

Behind a clear intention is a powerful imagination—an imagination so vast it aligns our heart and soul with the divine energies of creation—expanding well beyond the hologram we think we see. Many wondrous teachers and philosophers have been fascinated by the alluring mystery of intention and imagination over the years. A universal truth that emanates from many teachings is the power we tap into when we wish for something with our whole heart and soul. The master manifestation teacher, Neville Goddard, referred to this phenomenon in many of his books as having a burning desire.[1] Another spiritual teacher who often talked about the wonders that flow into our lives from having a powerful inner desire was Wayne Dyer, who based his book, *The Power of Intention* upon this universal truth.[2] Living with a burning inner desire also happens to be one of the most profound messages in *The Richest Man in Babylon* by George Clason.[3]

When you set an intention, always ask yourself if you wish for it with all your heart. We gain incredible clarity when we truly wish for something to happen—on every level of our existence. If you're not sure of what you wish for, or not sure of your purpose, shower yourself in loving compassion, and ask your soul for guidance and insight. The answer will emerge through your heart.

When you listen to your heart you beautifully align yourself with your soul's vibration. Living in soul alignment helps you set pristine intentions that beautifully resonate with your higher purpose. Your heart is a direct portal to your soul, and an inner desire felt in your heart is a manifestation of your soul's dream.

If your dreams and wishes are not born in your heart, they are not in resonance with your soul, and thus not in alignment with who you are. The fulfillment of empty dreams will never make you feel complete. No matter how many grand dreams you fulfill, if they are not born in your heart, you will always feel like something is missing.

When you live in elegant soul alignment, you attract miraculous outcomes. You don't even need to know exactly what it is you really want. All you truly need is knowing how you'd like to *feel*—from a place of connected soul love. The rest will take care of itself. Of course, if you happen to do know what you want, it becomes even easier to imagine how you'd like to feel. The key to setting a powerful intention happens to be to *imagine* how you'd like to *feel*—in a grateful state of blissful soul alignment. This is where your dreams are ultimately fulfilled.

MIRACULOUS INTENTION

Children are truly awesome at imagining great things. A few years back my daughter wished for an American Girl doll with all her heart. I told her to imagine playing with it, and would you believe it: Later that very same day a friend of the family knocked on our door and surprised her with—you guessed it—an American Girl doll! She had cracked the code of not only wishing for the doll with all her heart, but also visualizing and imagining herself in a frequency where she already had the doll. She had transformed herself to be, live, and feel herself in that frequency. She embodied the wish, and believed it would appear with her whole heart and soul.

Another time she miraculously found a tiny baby tooth we had been looking for an entire afternoon. Suddenly it appeared in her palm as she opened up her hand. This is a remarkable illustration of how expectations have the power of nudging outcomes in our desired direction. Children's abilities to imagine great outcomes continue to astonish me over and over.

It's not just children who know about this secret power. Us grown-ups also have the power to imagine wondrous things. The problem is so many of us have lost our belief in our imaginary powers. As soon as we get a glimpse of this successful formula though, we soon begin to remember this ancient golden path. We have taken the first step into an alchemical crucible of transformation and manifestation.

Some years back I found myself in a financial setback, and I wasn't sure what to do to get my hopes back up. One day I happened to read that Jade plants bring an aura of abundance into a home. With excited determination I put my daughter in her stroller and walked across the street to our local flower shop, where I bought a Jade plant with green thick lustrous leaves. As I placed it in the kitchen, I visualized golden treasures flowing our way, and I felt so excited. The *very next day* I received a phone call from the company I worked for at the time, saying they had miscalculated exchange rates on my previous bonuses, and I consequently received an unexpected amount of money larger than I could have ever conceived of at the time! The moment I had felt abundant, the money appeared in my life.

Dreamy Affirmations for
IMAGINING WITH INTENTION

—◦⊙◦—

THE KEY

My imagination holds the key to where I want to be.

* * *

A CHILD'S WONDER

I have the wonder of a child.
My imagination is running wild.

* * *

MIRACLES

I make room for miracles in my life
by listening to how I feel
and knowing how I would love to feel.

* * *

IMAGINARY DESIGNER

I am an imaginary aligner,
some call me a dream life designer.

* * *

IMAGINE

As I imagine and believe, so it will be.

* * *

WHEN I IMAGINE

When I imagine how I would like to feel,
the Universe opens doors I didn't even know existed.

* * *

INTENTIONAL DREAMING

I am an intentional dreamer and believer.

* * *

THE POWER OF IMAGINATION

I have the power to imagine myself anywhere.

* * *

IMAGINE BLISS

I honor myself with moments of bliss.
Even if it just means closing my eyes for a minute
and imagining how I would love to feel.

PRACTICE 1: IMAGINE WITH INTENTION

(a) Close your eyes and imagine yourself in a place
you'd like to be, doing what you'd like to do.
Maybe you feel more drawn to one type of
experience over another. Perhaps it is a writing
project, a holiday, or a new home. Or maybe
you wish to experience a romantic relationship,

a scientific breakthrough, a business plan, or a musical or artistic masterpiece. Whatever your dream may be, just imagine how it feels to be in that energy vibration.

(b) Visualize a fairytale solution to any dilemma in your life. How would that feel? Practice mindful awareness and imagine you already feel this way.

(c) Read the affirmations above out loud. Once you feel truly miraculous, create your own affirmations that wondrously state how truly special you feel right now.

2

Dream and Believe

THE UNIVERSE OPENS new doors when you live with an open heart and dream with your soul. As you go through life, be grateful for dreams and imaginary adventures that fill you with an abundance of energy and limitless inspiration. A visit to an imaginary realm where your deepest wish has come true is a divine blessing. You are familiarizing your mind, body, and soul with how it feels to operate in this aligned frequency, and best of all, you are preparing yourself for higher levels of initiations on the sacred path of the soul awakening.

We have the power of realigning our present experience in a momentary instance, and this is how we consciously and lovingly navigate into higher realms. Don't just take my word for it—take a look at this passage from the Bible below.

"And Jesus said to him, If you can!
All things are possible for one who believes."
—*The Bible, ESV: Mark 9.23*[4]

It is not enough simply saying a wish. First ask yourself if the wish is aligned with your soul's dream. The answer will emerge in your heart. Making a choice to live a purposeful life in high vibration involves consciously making decisions that will help you on your soul growth. Once you know your wish is something your whole heart desires, make the wish in a deep state of gratitude, and *believe* it to be true.

Every experience you imagine and believe to be true has the power of also being *perceived* and *felt* as true on every level of your existence. Whatever it is you may be dreaming or imagining, your mind and body experience the same emotional and physical reactions and sensations as if it was actually happening to you in physical reality.

The most wondrous aspect of imagination, from a soul growth perspective, is that it's in this higher state of being, experiencing, and visualizing that the marvelous energies expand. Here you are free from the constraints of physical reality and empowered to create wonders in a world with unlimited possibilities. Whatever your dreams may be, always remember to imagine and create in alignment with your soul—and *believe* in what you imagine.

In my mid-twenties I spent a few magnificent years in Australia. I lived in a cute little studio apartment on the water, overlooking the Sydney Harbour Bridge. Living there was a dream come true for me. The moment the plane touched down at Sydney Kingsford Smith airport I shed silent tears of deep gratitude. My parents had lived in Australia before I was born, and I had grown up longing to experience this magnificent place. My childhood home in Sweden was filled with boomerangs and precious corals, and I had a very cute koala bear made out of kangaroo skin in my room. Mostly I cherished listening to my parents' stories, and I could not get enough of hearing about when my mom swam in a lake filled with frogs and had to wade her hand to clear the way, or when they drove in the sizzling heat for hours and were so thirsty their tongues felt like sandpaper, and how my mom had not been let in to the pub to drink water because she was a woman. With love in my heart I eagerly listened to how the radios were only playing traditional songs such as Waltzing Matilda during their first month in Australia, because a music distribution company had gone on strike. I loved hearing about the animals, the ocean, and the critters. It was just all so exotic.

I made a decision already as a young child I would live there myself one day, and I believed it to be true. *My dream was clear*—I knew what I wanted, and from all the stories I had heard I knew how I wanted to feel, and *I felt it with my whole body and soul,* and *I believed it would happen with all my heart*—so it did. I moved to Sydney when I was twenty-two years old.

As serendipity would have it, it was in Sydney that I was blessed with one of my first guidance dreams. The sacred dream message that was relayed to me was very powerful, and as with most lessons in life, I believe it came to me because I was ready to hear it. Now, more than twenty years later, I can see how this truth came to serve as a building stone for the foundation of life as I know it. In the dream I found myself under water. I could breathe effortlessly, and felt invigorated and alive by the experience. Then it suddenly dawned on me that I should not be able to breathe under water, and I panicked. That very same moment I could no longer breathe. A voice in the dream then shared this beautiful message with me:

> Your mind cannot differentiate between
> what you think you are experiencing,
> and what you are experiencing.
> What you believe you can do,
> You can do.

Believe, and so it shall be. In my dream, I had received this eternal universal truth, and somehow aligned myself with this frequency. Because I was ready to receive this truth, my dreams helped me get there. The ancient Zen proverb, "*When the student is ready, the teacher will appear,"* beautifully conveys how our masters mysteriously show up at the right time. Masters can appear in our dreams, or as people acting as teachers in our lives. Rest assured, when your consciousness is rising, you notice an inflow of messages and guidance both in your dreams and daily life, and you also become aware of master teachers all around.

In our dreams we are able to fully align ourselves with the level of consciousness needed for our dreams to be fulfilled. That is why we want to take careful steps to calm our mind, and achieve a state of clear believing before drifting off to sleep. When we enter our dreams already in this higher state, we consequently do not need to waste precious dreamtime clearing away unwanted worries and emotional energies. Instead, as we begin dreaming, we can now go right to work, and embark on the dream of our dreams.

Dreamy Affirmations for
DREAMING AND BELIEVING

BELIEVE
What I believe I am experiencing,
I am experiencing.

* * *

EMPOWERMENT
What I believe I can do,
I can do.

* * *

OMNIPRESENT
I am omnipresent.

* * *

MY LITTLE DREAM
Little dream of mine,
Now I believe in you,
Thank you for awakening my divine,
and showing me dreams come true.

* * *

A NEW REALITY

I create a new reality,
by imagining it,
feeling it,
believing it,
and living in it.

* * *

THE ORACLE

I listen to the voice of the oracle
my visions and dreams are near.
Time has come for a miracle
There is nothing more to fear.

———◦⟨◦⟩◦———

PRACTICE 2: DREAM AND BELIEVE

(a) When you imagine with your heart, there is
no limit to what you can achieve. Read the
affirmations in this chapter out loud, and believe
in your words.

(b) Spend a few minutes breathing compassionately.
When you feel peaceful and serene, gratefully feel
your dream in your heart, and believe it to be
true.

(c) Imagine how it feels on every dimension of your
life, now that your dream has come true.

3

Interpret Your Dreams

EVERY DREAM YOU dream has the power of illuminating your imaginary powers of creation. Building a
celestial connection with your dreams, and embracing
them as sacred messengers, is one of the most beautiful
things you can do for yourself on your journey of soul
growth.

There is unlimited potential for practicing mindfulness when you listen to your dreams, and there is no
better practice ground to experience life from different
perspectives, and raising your awareness. Formless and
timeless, your dreams are omnipresent and vibrate with
an abundance of guidance and sacred messages. When
you truly take the time to connect with your dreams,
you soon see patterns emerging and evolving.

The best guidance you can ever receive is the
one you feel in your heart when you awaken from
your dreams. Your dreams communicate to you in

symbols—all carefully chosen to represent something to you. Mindful dreamwork helps you notice what you're really feeling and thinking—so you can address these thought patterns and improve them. Dreams of clarity sparkle like diamonds. A clear dream helps you view your experiences from a higher perspective, and brings about a luminous glow to situations that previously felt dark and dull.

Your dreams can be a source of immense creativity, and provide you with solutions you could not have thought of in your daily state of consciousness. As much fun as it is to decode our nightly dream adventures, it needs to be remembered though that some dreams were never meant to be interpreted. Some dreams, such as precious soul dreams, sometimes flow into your life just so you can experience, cherish, and honor the connection with your soul's home. If you are interested in exploring your dreams further, I write more about how to work with your own dreams in my first book, *Dream Guidance*.[5]

Dream guidance can give us a little nudge in the right direction just when we need it the most. The good news is that you can ask your dreams for guidance every night. The notion of asking your dreams for guidance, healing, and clarity is an ancient practice known as dream incubation. Whatever it is you wish to receive guidance about, you have a much higher chance of receiving illuminating messages when you are clear and specific with your question. Before drifting off to sleep, set a clear intention to dream about an answer to a particular situation in your life. Upon awakening, write down anything you can remember. I recommend continuing the incubation for a few more nights if the message is not immediately crystal clear. Your dreams will continue to help you find the answer by providing you with different examples, and giving you alternative ways of looking at the situation.

One person I would have loved to have met in person is Edgar Cayce, the renowned sleeping prophet. Edgar Cayce was able to tap into a field of answers and solutions by going into a trans-like sleeping state. In this deep state he was able to access something he referred to as the Akashic Records, or the book of life. Cayce described the Akashic Records as a movie of anything that has ever happened to all souls since creation, including what could happen in the future –with a mixture of ever-changing possibilities that depend on how we apply what we have learnt in the present moment.[6] Cayce often emphasized that it was not important what we had once been or done, but rather what we choose to focus on in the present moment, and how we deal with the challenges we face right here and now—knowing what we know now.

We all have things we wish we could have handled differently. The good news is we can all make better choices today, with the consciousness we have now—and that is what ultimately matters. Each experience in life is an opportunity for us to grow into better people and evolve as more conscious souls.

Dreamy Affirmations for
INTERPRETING YOUR DREAMS

———⟡———

COMPLETE LIFE

My life is complete
when I embrace my dreams

* * *

DREAM LIFE

When I find myself in dissonance,
I remind myself it's not always how it seems,
to live my life in resonance,
I listen closely to my dreams

* * *

A REMNANT OF A DREAM

A beautiful piece of art
the remnant of a dream
lives in my heart

* * *

AN ANGEL'S GRACE

In the early morning hours
little bells are ringing in my head
My room is filled with golden light
I look up and see tiny glistening stars above my bed

There is light everywhere around
The world is a loving place
I've been touched by an angel's grace.

PRACTICE 3: INTERPRET YOUR DREAMS

(a) Ask your dreams for guidance on a particular situation in your life before going to bed tonight. The answer will be in your dreams upon awakening.

(b) Honor the messages in your dreams. If you receive a clear sign in your dreams, listen to the message, and *act* on it.

(c) Create your own dream dictionary by writing down the associations you have to symbols in your dreams. The best dream dictionary is always the one you write yourself.

4

Dream with Your Soul

When you make a conscious choice
to live every moment of the day
in a state of expanded awareness,
you mindfully flow through the day,
and everything turns out okay.

YOUR DREAMS CONNECT you with an immense field of wisdom, creativity, and infinite love, and embracing your dreams is like an incredible love dance with your soul. Living, dreaming, and dancing in flow *is* a conscious choice, and it is yours to make every day. It is a choice you make every morning upon awakening, a choice you make throughout the day, and most importantly, it is a choice you make at the end of each day.

In the Tibetan practice of Dream Yoga, it is widely honored that the state of consciousness you go to sleep with is also the consciousness you carry with you into dreamland. The Tibetan Buddhists honor their consciousness in all that they do, and the goal of this ancient practice is total enlightenment. As opposed to many other views and philosophies on sleep, particularly in the West where we tend to view sleep primarily as a time for achieving deep rest, Tibetan practitioners of Dream Yoga think of sleep as a monumental time for deepening their spiritual practice, and careful attention is therefore placed on achieving a clear level of consciousness before drifting off to sleep.[7]

When you take the time to mindfully reflect upon your day, you declutter some of the emotional debris, illusions, and unnecessary thoughts that have accumulated in your head. You elegantly raise your awareness, and when you fall asleep more of your sleeping hours can now be dedicated to deepen and further your spiritual growth, rather than working through emotional clutter. This enhanced awareness opens up an abundance of opportunities for clarity and infinite wisdom, making your dreams serve as a university of higher consciousness and soul growth.

SOUL DREAMING

When you begin to listen more closely to your dreams, it is often helpful to view them from different perspectives. Dreams are multi-dimensional in nature, and layers of messages and insights can often be found within one and the same dream. From one angle, our dreams can be seen as emotional processing generators. These types of dreams help us grow on a personal level, helping us reach better self-knowledge and understanding about ourselves, and gaining deeper insight about the way we interact with people around us. Emotional processing dreams can be viewed as showcasing a holographic representation of our current psyche, and as created by the mind—our projector.

From a broader angle, we can also look at some of our dreams as not originating in our mind, but rather in a different realm. These are our soul dreams. In a soul dream, you expand into a higher frequency and experience dreams that help you grow on a timeless soul level. This is where you awaken to the dream of your soul, and begin to experience a higher consciousness in divine alignment. You may be presented with soul initiations, be invited to explore faraway places, and ultimately guided to transcend into a higher frequency all together. Some soul dreams connect you with dream guides or loved ones, others enlighten you with sacred messages. All soul dreams fill you with an endless sense of love with a deep connection to the infinity of the dream. Soul dreams tend to come about only after we first begin to work on our awareness in daily life, undertaking both subjective and objective analysis of ourselves, with honest self-reflection from a higher perspective—and above all, engaging in a daily meditation practice.

In Australia, many Aboriginal groups have been known to engage in sacred soul dreaming—where their soul travels in the night. The Mardu people, an Aboriginal group up in the western Kimberley region of Australia, often talk about their dream-spirit leaving their body during dreams. Trips and journeys undertaken in these dreams are all considered very real.[8] Another Aboriginal group, also in the western part of Australia, the Pintupi Aboriginals, tell of similar experiences, where their spirits may meet with ancestral figures, and how they may also receive special knowledge in the dream, including songs and rituals that may otherwise have been lost to the people.[9]

This timeless connection that Aboriginals have been making during their dream travels for tens of thousands of years can be thought of as a celestial experience within an infinite field. Carl Jung often talked about the sacred experience of aligning our goals with the infinite, rather than placing our focus on meaningless possessions, as the latter types of goals would always be limited and restricted in nature.[10] Jung even went as far as saying that a person's level of satisfaction in life depends on his or her relation to the infinite.

It is this very connection with the infinite we all cherish so much, whenever we get a glimpse of it. The golden field we tap into when meditating and dreaming is infinite, and our soul is timeless. With a devoted meditation and mindfulness practice, you will raise your awareness in your waking life, and enhance your chances of having more fulfilling soul dreams in the night, beautifully expanding into this timeless field. Going to bed with a clear intention of dreaming with clarity is the most powerful step you can take to achieve this goal. When you enter your dreams with a sacred state of consciousness you form a celestial connection with a higher realm—the golden field of your soul's home.

Dreamy Affirmations for
DREAMING WITH YOUR SOUL

—◦◦◦◦◦—

IMAGINARY ALIGNMENT
I align my imagination with my dreams.

* * *

DREAMS
When I honor my dreams
I see how guided, loved and connected I am.

* * *

I AM THE DREAM
I am an old soul
I am awareness
I am always here,
always have been,
and always will be.
I'm the dream that guides,
I'm the hug that loves,
I'm the light that shines.

* * *

THE GOLDEN RAINBOW
There is a golden rainbow in my dream,
a golden rainbow on the meadow;

and everywhere I go today,
life is flowing like a dream.

* * *

MINDFUL

It is truly delightful,
how my dreams just flow
when I am mindful.
Long before day break,
I am wonderfully awake.

* * *

GOODNIGHT FROGS

When I go to bed,
I whistle a lullaby,
and say goodnight
to all little frogs in my head.

—⚬⟡⚬—

PRACTICE 4: IMAGINING YOUR DREAMS

(a) When you to go bed tonight, mindfully reflect
upon your day and enter a peaceful golden light
meditation.

(b) When you feel your energy expanding, set a clear
intention of dreaming clear soul dreams.

(c) Say a dream affirmation of your choice as you
enter dreamland.

(d) Every night from now on, before you fall asleep, practice a brief meditation, say your affirmation, and feel and believe it to be true as your drift into the golden field of your soul's eternal home.

5

Dream of Possibilities

IN THE WORLD of quantum physics everything is thought of as being made up of subatomic particles that exist in a "wave state", or as pure potential when not observed.[11] In his book, *Our Mathematical Universe*, Max Tegbrand talks about how everything is not what it seems, and eloquently writes about how two particles could in fact appear in two places at once, leading to what's known as a quantum conundrum, and possibly even parallel universes.[12]

There might very well be an infinite number of timelines and possible paths and futures available to us—to observe. One of my favorite authors, Dr. Joe Dispenza, talks about how wave state theory applies to everything in our physical reality, and describes how everything is in fact pure potential, even possible futures.[13]

We each perceive reality based on our subjective awareness, and if we take into account all the recent developments in quantum physics it is indeed possible that we could be getting glimpses of scenes that are really all happening at once. There is no better practice ground for experiencing and observing different possibilities and alternative scenes than in your dreams. In contrast to waking reality, where events are viewed in a linear time line, in your dreams you no longer experience this barrier. Here you are free to create and explore, and try out different waves of possibilities. Upon awakening, you can then more consciously observe the possibility that best resonates with your inner soul dream.

Dream journeys offer you timeless guidance and wisdom. If there is no such thing as time, and we are able to truly experience this ultimate reality in our dreams, the journeys and encounters we have in our dreams are definitely something worth treasuring and reflecting upon. When you dream you are not confined by the regular constraints of daily life, so there are infinite opportunities to explore possibilities, and this includes experiencing the present moment outside of time and space. In your dreams you can revisit past events, get glimpses of what's to come, explore and try out new experiences and possible solutions, go on faraway journeys, and meet with loved ones who may have transitioned.

DREAMTIME

As we saw in the previous chapter, the Australian Aboriginals have lived and dreamed timelessly for as long as can be conceived. One of the oldest and richest cultures of the world, the Australian Aboriginals view "waking" reality as only one type of experienced reality. They believe we experience another reality in Dreamtime—the timeless realm which according to this sacred tradition is where everything was created, where we've come from, and will return.[14] In the Aboriginal tradition, Dreamtime is as real as this reality. Dreamtime was long ago, and at the same time it keeps on living in the present, and can be revisited and reconnected to, through dream journeys on the land, and can also be entered through meditation, nighttime dreams, and initiations.[15]

Timeless dreaming also used to have a central place in the lives of the Hopi Indians, who lived in northeastern Arizona. They had a timeless language, in which there were no terms for past, present, and future. According to Marie Louise von Franz, they viewed the universe as having two aspects: that which is already manifest, and that which is beginning to manifest. Any physical object in the world is already manifested, whereas anything internal, such as images, feelings and expectations, relate more to the future. Rather than viewing time as continuously flowing, the Hopi viewed their reality as having distinguished moments.[16]

In North America, the Iroquois placed special emphasis on dream travel, and often undertook extensive travels within their dreams to receive guidance from the future. Robert Moss, who has studied the traditions of the Iroquois in great detail, describes how they were very gifted dreamers who often sought help from each other, and how they would go back inside a dream to gain even more clarity. The Iroquois also assigned dream scouts to travel in their dreams, to locate enemies, or find good places for hunting. In the morning, they then gathered around and listened to the dreams.[17]

Dreamy Affirmations for
DREAMING OF POSSIBILITIES

———⚬◦⊙◦⚬———

DREAM MAKING
I imagine the possibility,
and believe it to be true,
This my dear friend,
is how I make my dreams come true.

* * *

CONSCIOUSNESS
Consciousness is vast
it's never my past

* * *

MAKING A NEW START
I focus all my vibrant energy
on opportunities that best serve me
I listen to my heart,
there is nothing wrong in making a new start.

* * *

TAKE THE LEAP
I listen to my heartbeat,
there is no question,

it's time to take the leap,
my soul is yearning for expression!

———◦⟨⟨⟩⟩◦———

PRACTICE 5: DREAMING OF POSSIBILITIES

(a) When you go to bed tonight, set a clear intention to embrace a younger version of yourself in your dreams. As your drift off to sleep, feel love and compassion in your heart, for the younger version of your soul.

(b) When you wake up in the morning, spend some time connecting with the Universe. Feel the loving rays of the sun, the warmth of the earth, the protection of the mountains, the life force of the trees. Imagine yourself in a place of high vibrations. You're literally on top of the world. Now expand your energy and become one with the cosmos. From here, visualize an opportunity you would like to happen. Bring this vision with you when you rise today, and now keep focusing your energy in this direction.

6

Flow in Gratitude

GRATITUDE IS A wonderful energy vibration. When you live in gratitude and flow in the here and now, your life unfolds like a dream. You have the power of the Universe behind you, within you, and around you. Whenever you experience gratitude for what you have, you are instantly brought back into the present, and in this loving vibration you attract even more golden moments to be grateful for into your life—and you guessed it, this does wonders to your imagination and dream fulfillment abilities.

A lovely way to expand the smooth vibration of gratitude, is devoting yourself to a daily gratitude practice. Perhaps your practice involves writing little notes of gratitude and placing them in a glass jar, or maybe collecting grateful thoughts in a journal as you go to bed each night. Or you may begin the day with expressing your gratitude for at least ten things in your life every morning. It is not important how you practice gratitude, what matters for your soul connection is that you do it. Living in gratitude is one of the most beautiful ways of aligning yourself with your soul's home, and living with higher purpose. Every moment you experience gratitude, you hold the golden key to flowing with your soul.

Your heart has a celestial resonance, and when fully open it vibrates in perfect alignment with your soul's home—in the eternal now. One of the most brilliant aspects of flowing in the moment is that we get to participate in our journey wholly and fully. The seeds for your life are planted in this very present moment. What you choose to think about right now expands. Every thought, action, and reaction today will impact how you experience life tomorrow. Your door to infinite wisdom is found right here in the only moment there ever is—right now. There is only ever one now, and that is now. Imagining and visualizing what you wish for—from a frequency of love and gratitude, in the here and now, is like planting miraculous seeds in an enchanting garden. Your little garden will grow into an oasis in paradise, in divine harmony.

By living in a state of wonder and gratitude you become more and more aware of miracles as they flow into your life, which in turn helps you experience even more gratitude. The truth is miracles do happen. They come in all shapes and sizes, and can be found all around us. We live in a world filled with enchanting energies.

A life in gratitude flows with awe. An event may be expected on some levels, but on others it's truly remarkable it happened at all, and overall it is a miracle. Whenever something good flows your way, be sure to express your gratitude. You are now in a miraculous vibration of divine soul alignment.

Some imaginary beings who know about the power of experiencing joy and gratitude in the present moment are my friends: *The Dancing Elephants.* One day during one of my imaginary travels I stumbled upon a remarkable image: On the middle of the African savannah, there were elephants of all sizes dancing away:

> There was once a small cabana
> on the African savanna
> where elephants ruled the way,
> keeping all prey at bay
> by dancing all day.

Why are they dancing? You may ask. The blissful truth is, the elephants are dancing because they know that being in a state of joy and gratitude does not only bring them happiness in the present moment, but this wondrous feeling also helps them transcend into a higher frequency where they are less likely to attract situations that are not for their highest good.

We can all learn from the dancing elephants. The elephants are dancing away to remind us to live in a frequency of laughter and play—which not only keeps the prey away, but also helps us to beautifully seize each day. When we live in passionate flow, we live with an open heart, and whatever we decide to do is made from a place of soul alignment.

Dreamy Affirmations for
FLOWING IN GRATITUDE

———•⟨⟨⟩⟩•———

GRATEFUL MIRACLES
I practice gratitude each day
and see miracles flow my way.

* * *

SPIRITUAL WEALTH
Gratitude for my physical health
brings on an attitude of spiritual wealth.

* * *

A DANCING ELEPHANT
I am a dancing elephant.
I flow in joy,
living here and now.

* * *

THANK YOU
Thank you my inner divine,
for helping me stay aligned,
purposeful and kind.

* * *

FLOWING IN GRATITUDE
When gratitude flows,
magic grows.

* * *

THE BLISS OF NOW
When each moment is treasured
as a sacred now
I no longer live in confinement
because my heart, mind, and soul,
are now in blissful alignment

* * *

STEP INTO THE PRESENT
I step into the present, and out of the past.

* * *

SOUL RHYTHM
My heart beats to the
rhythm of my soul.

* * *

OPEN HEART
When I live and flow with an open heart,
every day is off to a great start.

* * *

A HYMN TO MY BODY

I may just be passing through
but there is never a doubt
my existence in this realm
depends on you.
You are my temple
I honor you
thank you for hosting me
I love you.

PRACTICE 6: FLOW IN GRATITUDE

(a) Read the grateful affirmations above clearly and
confidently. Feel them and say them out loud
until you feel sparkles of grateful joy in your heart.

(b) Imagine a blissful experience that would bring
about a feeling you would love to have in your
heart. Now set an intention that it has already
happened, and experience gratitude in your heart.

(c) Write your own notes of gratitude to express
gratitude for at least ten things in your life. The
more the better. Let the gratitude flow, and see the
magic grow.

7

Cherish Wisdom

EVERY REMARKABLE INVENTION in the world was once born inside the imaginary realms of a highly inspired person. Living with the intention to learn something new every day does wonders for your own inspiration and imaginary flow.

Wisdom beautifully enriches your soul, fills you with immense inspiration, and brings about an inner desire to create. It's exciting to look at your life as a big university. Plan your own curriculum and write summaries of what you read. If you ponder on questions as you peruse new literature, write them down in your journal. The questions can be used as tickets for your imaginary quests and creations. When you strive to learn something new every day, you also keep boredom away. When you want something, you make the time for it, and believe me—you will feel eternally rewarded when enriching your life with knowledge.

There is an abundance of books for every problem ever encountered in the world. Whatever it is you're going through at this moment in time, you can rest assured there are other people who have experienced that very situation before you—and that there is a wide selection of books that would speak directly to your heart right now. By making an intention to find soul enriching books, you will soon have a whole library filled with books that you feel connected with. Books awaken ideas, and help us learn from one another. Ultimately books help us build a deeper sense of community.

If you treasure wisdom, and love *reading* and *listening* to inspiring words by great thinkers, inventors, imaginary creators, and beautiful souls—you're already a step ahead on your imaginary journey. Oh, and you read that right—books can also be *listened* to. The benefits of actually reading the carefully chosen words by a beloved writer cannot be underestimated. It's a truly magical feeling seeing magnificent words come to life inside a rustic hardcover book. That being said, if you are also interested in feeding your imagination with ideas, sparks, and fireflies, then listening to books work just as well.

The elegant truth is that reading serves as super food for our imagination. We can set off on an imaginary adventure and actually *feel* we're there. We have the power to imagine ourselves anywhere. That very same feeling you get when setting foot in a new place can be imagined—and relived anywhere.

There is a mountain of good soul enriching books out there. When you find authors you resonate with, read all their books, and also do some research to see which books may have inspired them along the way. Chances are you share the same exquisite taste of both fiction and non-fiction. As a note of caution, always be sure to exercise discernment when choosing what books or texts to read. The same of course applies to movies and TV shows. You would not wish to lower your vibrational field with by bombarding yourself with negative ideas, thought forms, and dark energies.

Over the years, I've deepened my wisdom and fueled my passion for spirituality, psychology, dreams, crystals, numerology, feng shui, and yoga, along with spiritual traditions from Christianity and Tibetan Buddhism. I aim to live each day in creative flow, and have found that meditating, reading, writing, and dreaming are my muses in life.

When you live in soul alignment, you can rest assured whatever spiritual avenue or practice you feel drawn to on your own journey of soul growth is the path for you.

Dreamy Affirmations for
CHERISHING WISDOM

STAY CURIOUS

Staying curious to life's mysteries,
fuels my inspiration and creativity.
Meeting each day with wonder
is the key to staying cognizant and smart
and this is how I live everyday
young at heart.

* * *

DAILY PRACTICE

Life may come with many tests
but it's my daily practice that brings true success.

* * *

ENRICHMENT

I honor my inner quest,
and enrich my life with knowledge.
My life is eternally blessed.

PRACTICE 7: CHERISHING WISDOM

(a) Learn something new today, and commit yourself
to reading or listening to more books.

(b) With gratitude in your heart, write your own affirmations that embrace your love for wisdom.

(c) Live your wisdom, and share your knowledge with the world.

8

Write in Morning Glory

THE EARLY MORNING hours flow with the smooth vibration of stillness. When you give yourself at least a few minutes of blissful peace every morning you get to experience this serene energy. Even waking up just thirty minutes earlier than usual can pave the way for a graceful wave flowing into your life. It is also in the early morning that your mind is most tuned in. There is no going around it, most of us just think quicker and sharper in the morning, and whatever we do is simply done with so much more efficiency, grace, and clarity.

It is in the morning that you are most receptive to brilliant ideas and eloquent epiphanies, and if you are in tune with your soul's vibration, these ideas have the power to not only help you fulfill your own soul dream, but also those of other souls. Honor your sleep like the holy grail, and avoid watching news or any kind of

TV shows right before going to sleep. A good night's sleep will help you wake up feeling aware, inspired, and happy in your heart. When you prioritize the quality of your sleep no matter where you are, or what you do—you develop a beautiful habit of not only going to bed and waking up at the same time every day of the week, but you also end up keeping a healthier diet. This may even include avoiding alcohol all together, if you find it impacts the quality of your sleep, or that it influences your presence when awake. Unless you are going to an Oscar's awards gala or are invited to attend the most extraordinary event of the century, there is no need to stay up late even in the weekends. If you are meeting friends for dinner, say you would like to have dinner early. If you make it a habit of always going to bed by no later than 9 P.M., you will smoothly wake up by yourself at 5 A.M.—no alarm required.

FIND YOUR MORNING SONG

If you have a hard time getting up in the morning, remember it tends to be more motivating to be an early riser when you have a project you feel passionate about—especially in the darker months of the year. When you are inspired, you want to rise early, and share your song with the world, just as a little bird.

Writing is a loving state of creative clarity, and in this unconstrained state you can compose miraculous prose and create enchanting affirmations straight from your heart. The more you write and engage in any kind of creative flow, the more time you'll spend in this wondrous place of soul flow. Explore the idea of writing an affirmation or two every morning. Do this practice for at least a few weeks, and see how you feel. The affirmations and writings you love the most, you can then print out in large font, or draw in pencil and place around the house. Chances are you are going to be reaping some feel-good success rewards. It is also in this vibrational frequency of creation that you really begin to flow.

I truly love writing in the early morning hours. That's when I feel most connected. When I write, I am fully aligned with my highest source of inspiration, and in this sacred moment I am one with the divine, my highest self, my soul, my heart, my mind, and my memories.

Honoring your connection with your dreams and writing them down in a journal every morning is a great way of nourishing the connection with your soul, and keeping ideas flowing. It's not only a wonderful way to start the day, but it also enhances the flow between your unconscious and conscious—and hence boosts your imagination even more!

As a young girl I began a tradition of writing my dreams from one side of the journal, and my daily reflections from the other side of the journal. This is a practice I warmheartedly recommend. This is your imaginary bible. All your dreamy adventures, daily reflections, and imaginary travels bundled together in one golden collection.

Whether you keep a hardcover journal wrapped in romantic ancient maps or take notes on your phone, the fact that you're honoring your insights and jotting down words is awesome. I carry a notebook with me at all times, and love taking it out whenever inspiration strikes. This way I can easily pencil down thoughts, ideas, and marvelous imaginations on the go. While writing my spiritual memoir, *The Dream Alchemist,* I probably reached more knowledge about myself than I had in a whole lifetime.[18] As I was writing down my experiences, soon enough patterns and unconscious habits began to emerge, which in turn helped me view myself with more love, compassion, and understanding—and above all, reverence for my soul.

Even though the process of connecting with yourself on a deeper level can be tough, trying, and exhausting, the practice of writing down your self-reflective insights and revelations opens the lid to a brilliant treasure box. The golden gift of loving ourselves has no monetary value.

Dreamy Affirmations for
WRITING IN MORNING GLORY

MORNING GLORY
I wake with a smile on my face
it's time to tell a story
I find my sacred space
writing in morning glory.

* * *

EARLY TO RISE
I am early to rise
healthy and wise.

* * *

MY TIME
The first part of the morning
is mine to keep.

* * *

WRITER'S LAND
I dream of adventures in writer's land
and maybe one or two visits to fairyland.

* * *

SLEEP TIGHT
When I stay away from the blue light,
my night is all right.

* * *

MY INNER DESIRE WILL TAKE ME HIGHER
I honor my inner desire
because it is within my heart
I find the strength to go higher.

* * *

GOOD MORNING
Good morning,
rise and shine
do a little twirl
I embrace my divine
it's time to greet the world.

* * *

WONDROUS MORNING
Welcome wondrous morning,
Oh, how I've awaited your soft shine, so bright
You make everything so brilliantly clear;
No matter how long the night;
Like a blossoming flower,
you gracefully transform my fear,
to love, light, and power.

* * *

MY STORY

My dreams are coming true.
I love writing my story.

———⚬⚬⚬———

PRACTICE 8. WRITE IN MORNING GLORY

(a) When you go to bed tonight, set the intention
to awaken early, and to clearly remember your
dreams. Upon awakening, connect with your
dream, and recount it before starting to move
around. Then reach out for your journal and
record whatever image emerges.

(b) Read the affirmations in this chapter out loud and
visualize yourself in a loving creative state in the
early hours of the morning. When you're there,
write your own affirmations and express gratitude
for feeling so connected in the morning.

(c) Get up 30 minutes earlier for the next ten
days, and write for at least twenty minutes each
morning.

9

Look for the Silver Lining

TRUTH BE TOLD, it can be hard to imagine good outcomes in the midst of setbacks. When failure comes around, the inner bliss of loving perfection that you once felt could soon feel like a long-lost memory. When you're in a thick foggy daze, it can be hard to see the path in front of you, and it can be a daunting task to say the least to try to view something optimistically.

From time to time we all get weighed down with emotional stress, fears, and limiting beliefs. Even though road blocks could very well signal that you're out of alignment or simply not on the right path, it would not be right to view all setbacks in a negative light. Sometimes setbacks bring about opportunities that ultimately help us reach even higher levels of understanding. Experiencing sad situations can turn into loving learning experiences for consciously evolving and growing. In his incredible autobiography, *A Long Walk to Freedom,*[19] Nelson Mandela beautifully talks about his own soul growth during the decades of his imprisonment. In the midst of suffering he focused on living a life in full expression. He honored his health and started every morning by running in place inside his small cell. He cherished knowledge and read and learned anything he could get his hands on. He loved connecting with other captives, and built a strong community wherever he went; and every day he would write about his experiences and insights in a secret journal. Throughout the years, he kept his vision for his country, and when he was finally freed, he helped his people by becoming the Prime Minister of South Africa.

Nelson Mandela was a man who persisted in his vision for his country, no matter what happened around him. This is the beauty of impediments. Sometimes when things don't go your way you realize how much you truly want something. In fact, when hindrances help you see what you don't want, you can then better focus on what you do want. Failure has an amazing ability to help you develop more clarity.

FAILURE HAPPENS TO
SHOW THE WAY

It is the immense energy of the clarity that follows failure that has the power of transforming your wishes into action. Setbacks can be lessons in faith and focus, and can hold the answer to your destiny. Difficult life circumstances have the power of awakening us with a jolt. If we allow ourselves to tap into the immense energies that follow and embrace the experiences instead of drowning from them, we have the opportunity to rise and grow with any situation—and ultimately find ourselves in higher frequencies.

By learning to accept where we are—and understand our experiences with compassion—we learn to love ourselves, and begin to see life through a more loving lens. This is an opportune moment for us to pause briefly and make an important differentiation between material success and vibrational success. As alluring and enchanting it may be to embark on luxury travels, and own beautiful homes, cars and clothes, the higher purpose that we're primarily talking about in this book, is living on a higher frequency of existence. If you also happen to attract material success along the way, that's just a nice side benefit.

HOPE

Some setbacks are caused by illusion. The good news is that with an enlightened perspective illusion dissolves. The moment you decide to look for the silver lining, the light appears. In fact, it is through the very act of looking for the silver lining that we move through energies, rather than being stuck in them. Through the years I have found that having hope is worth as much as gold in the bank, if not more. No matter how hopeless or trapped we feel—praying for help, and looking at the event as a learning experience, ultimately help us transcend the plateau. Your light will come back—sometimes brighter than you had even dreamed of.

A few years back I received some news that were rather challenging, and I felt hopeless. I had no control over the situation and just didn't know how to solve the problem. After spending a few days feeling sorry for myself, I knew very well that this was not the answer. The time had come to turn to my dreams for guidance and direction. I ended up having a dream that helped lift me to a more empowered place. In my dream, I met and embraced one of my most beloved spiritual teachers. It was a very loving encounter, filled with happiness, but most of all, in the dream I felt the teacher's appreciation and immense gratitude for what I do. This dream helped expand my consciousness into a more loving frequency. When I realized it was time to handle the dilemma in a different manner, my hope immediately came back. In my dream I had received the energy I needed to get back on my feet and take on the assignment with a new attitude. The situation had not changed, but my heart was open, and I had remembered my soul alignment. Now I had a new vision. The best way to handle a dilemma is to consciously expand into a higher frequency, and meet your old problems with a new level of consciousness.

Some of the verses below are not affirmations in a traditional sense, but rather poetic, ruminative reflections. They are included in this chapter, as they sing with the essence of hope. By looking for the silver lining whenever you experience despair, hope will come.

Dreamy Ruminations on
LOOKING FOR THE SILVER LINING

—◦⟨◦⟩◦—

I FOUND MYSELF IN MY HEART

It was when everything fell apart
that I found myself in my heart.

* * *

THE GIRL WITH THE SILVER LINING

Living on nickels a day,
some might say her world has gone gray
but she keeps smiling
her nickels have a silver lining.

* * *

A LITTLE LOVE POEM TO MY FAIRY

How I wonder where you are
little fairy of the night
You came and shined so bright
and told me it's all right.

* * *

THE GIRL WHO LIVED ON AIR

Have you ever heard of the girl,
who lived on air,
and had miracles appear everywhere?

She could move the world
and was never once in despair
Boy, do I wish she were here.

* * *

THAT'S WHY IT HURTS
A panic attack feels like labor pain in the chest
because something is trying to emerge
That's why it hurts.

* * *

THE BREAKUP
I knew the day would come
I've been ready to move on
but now that I am here
there is nothing more I fear
than to walk this road alone.

* * *

SETBACKS
I am grateful for my setbacks,
because each one has helped me choose
a more loving and connected path.

* * *

SOMETIMES WE DON'T KNOW WHY
When I learn to embrace a sad situation
with the wisdom that I don't know why
it feels a little brighter.

* * *

SOMETIMES ALL YOU NEED IS REST
When your soul feels lost
and the nights as dark as coal
ask yourself
Is this part of my quest?
Or is it perhaps a test?
But never forget dear soul
sometimes all you need is rest.

* * *

A NEW DAY
Whenever I feel discomfort
over something I said,
or did not say,
I remind myself it's okay
Tomorrow is a new day.

PRACTICE 9: LOOK FOR THE SILVER LINING

(a) Think of a situation in your life that feels challenging. Imagine being a bird and now see yourself from a higher perspective. Is there a silver lining you may not yet have seen?

(b) Read the ruminations in this chapter out loud. Once you feel acceptance in your heart, close your eyes and create your own affirmation filled with hope, love, and gratitude.

(c) Be gentle with yourself during any times of setbacks. This is your time to heal and reconnect. Shower yourself with compassion.

10

Flow with Love

WAVES OF LOVE flow from a soul in divine alignment.

There are many paths to soul alignment. Practicing yoga is a transcendent experience that holds the golden key for dreaming, creating, and flowing into a life of full expression. Yoga teaches you to accept, surrender, and breathe through challenging circumstances, no matter what is happening within and around you, and has the power of bringing about a celestial shift in your life.

Stepping onto your yoga mat each day, even it's just for a few minutes, is a powerful ritual that helps harness your inner awareness and connection. The ancient Indian yogis tapped into this sacred wisdom thousands of years ago. For each time you move and breathe synchronously, you're elegantly training yourself to bring your attention to one thing at the time. Yoga aligns your mind, body, and soul with the Divine.

When you give yourself the gift of a daily yoga practice, you elegantly blossom into the radiant being of light that you are, and begin to achieve things you may once have thought of as impossible tasks. When you dream and imagine from a clear frequency of celestial alignment, the Universe supports your soul dream.

Practicing yoga with love in your heart helps you make conscious choices throughout the day, and imagine from a place of love and connection. Every day you have the choice to live in a state of love where your days are filled with compassion, connection, and clarity, or to live in a dazed state of fear where your mind is consumed by sporadic thoughts and intense emotional reactions. Yoga helps you tune into the frequency of your soul's home, and everything you do from this place is done with love.

With a devoted daily yoga, mindfulness, and meditation practice you will bring your awareness with you into your own dreamscape, and you will continue your practice of awakening while dreaming and sleeping. The dedication you show yourself by practicing yoga flows back into your life in a multitude of good ways. Yoga helps you build a deeper connection with your soul, people around you, and the entire Universe.

What I love most about yoga is the loving connection I feel in my heart when I practice. There is such precious lightness. I fell in love with yoga shortly after moving to California almost twenty years ago now. I knew I wanted to do yoga, but had no idea how to do it, so I signed myself up for a workshop in the adorable seaside village of Laguna Beach. As luck would have it, I was blessed with a profound experience my very first time ever practicing yoga. The teacher showed us how we could create energy fields that felt like loving spheres just by moving our hands. I was mesmerized, and yes, I kept creating these energy fields on a daily basis for years to come. The funny thing is, in all the thousands of yoga classes I've taken since then, including also having undergone my own yoga teacher training, I never once again encountered a teacher who taught this particular phenomenon. It was very serendipitous indeed that I was able to experience the infinite love of my own soul in my very first yoga class. It was meant to happen. It was time for my whole being to become aligned with my inner divine.

In traditional Kundalini yoga, there is an asana known as Sufi grinds, which happens to be one of my favorite practices of all. A few years ago, I had a powerful guidance dream where an angel showed me the art of entering new levels of existence by spinning my body. It wasn't until after I had this dream that I realized why I love this flowing movement so much. By moving in soft circles, we spin into higher energy levels, and this is where creation takes place. When we fully align ourselves with the divine energies of the Universe in this highly vibrational state, we are creating from a clear and pure state of consciousness, and there is just love. We have entered the golden field of divine consciousness and dream with our soul.

A daily yoga practice also leads to a more loving experience in the present moment. Living in love, in the present moment of now, is the most compassionate gift we can ever give our loved ones. When we are fully present, we are ready to serve the world. When you take the time to lovingly connect with people around you, the celestial energies expand, and you are brought to even higher frequencies. By reaching a higher consciousness, you will beautifully attract even more serendipity, synchronicity, and miraculous guidance into your life, and now you can truly be of service to the world.

Dreamy Affirmations for
FLOWING WITH LOVE

———◦◦◦———

FLOW AND GROW
When I'm flowing, I'm growing
I dream big and flow often.

* * *

SPIN
I spin into a higher existence of being.

* * *

SPIN INTO THE LIGHT
I acknowledge my fear.
Then I pray for a miracle
and spin into the light.

* * *

COMFORT ZONE
I am stepping out of my comfort zone,
because I am ready to experience a higher frequency.

* * *

STEP BY STEP
I make my dreams come true
step by step.

* * *

CLEAR INTENTIONS
I live and flow with clear intentions.

* * *

INTENTIONAL LIVING
For each intentional step I take,
I am honoring my soul by consciously transcending
into a higher reality of being, living, and dreaming.

* * *

LOVE AND SERVE
The more I love and serve,
The more I feel part of this world.

* * *

A GOLDEN SMILE
Wherever I go,
I greet people with love and affection,
I am so grateful for each sparkly connection
and every golden smile.
It's quite a collection.

* * *

LOVING GIVER
I am a loving giver and a grateful receiver.

PRACTICE 10: FLOW WITH LOVE

(a) Take a yoga class at a studio, or practice a few rejuvenating asanas at home. For every breath, honor your awareness and flow with love in your heart.

(b) Do something wonderful for one of your loved ones or friends today.

(c) Encourage someone to share a special story and listen with all your heart.

(d) Greet everyone you meet with a compassionate smile.

11

Meditate with Grace

TRANSFORMING OUR INNER state is the master key to ultimately reaching a state of pure consciousness from which we can co-create in golden alignment with the Universe. The notion of first working on our inner selves before we can change any outer situation happens to be an old ancient alchemical secret.

When we hear the word *alchemy*, it's common to first think of the more extroverted notions of alchemy in the Middle Ages, where the main focus of practitioners was on making gold out of base metals like iron and lead. But there was a more introverted group of alchemists already back in the third century who believed that outer transformation comes from first working on the inner state. One of those alchemists was Zosimos, a Greek alchemist who lived in Egypt. Zosimos listened closely to his dreams, and believed that the mystery of the universe could be found within ourselves. In the 16th century, the Belgian philosopher and alchemist Gerhard Dorn, believed it was necessary to reach a magical state within before anything could be transformed on the outside, and said that divine influence could easier be received after matter was first brought back into its original pure state. [20] The inner and outer paths of alchemy, were also present in ancient China, where extroverted alchemists initially sought magical elixirs in the quest for eternal life, and introverted alchemists believed more in the practice of inner spiritual practices.[21]

A sacred practice that helps bring us back into our original pure state is meditation. When we meditate, we softly float back into the golden infinite field of our soul's blissful home. Meditation brings us back to where we were all along. If you wish to live a more peaceful life, feel more centered, radiate with love and grace, have more energy, joy, awareness, and compassion—and above all connect with your soul's home in the golden field, dedicating even just a few minutes each day to meditation will do wonders.

The first time I experienced the immense love of this golden field when meditating, was during a spiritual satsang led by a woman who had just returned from India. The experience was so profound that it propelled me to travel to India and re-experience what I had just had a glimpse of, over and again. I spent a month in silence in a small ashram, meditating every day from early morning to late night. Ever since that blissful experience, I've kept and developed my own sacred meditation practice, and have witnessed first-hand the many miraculous reverberations that can be felt on all levels of our lives from keeping a devoted meditation practice. I write more about this sacred journey in my spiritual memoir, *The Dream Alchemist.*[22]

A few conscious breaths have the power of reconnecting you with your inner light, the sun of your soul. When you connect with the immense golden light that resides within you, something happens. Your eyes softly sparkle, and your skin begins to glow. You may have noticed this sacred sensation after a yoga class, or after a rejuvenating walk on the beach. This inner connection expands into divine wholeness. You are vibrating with an all-encompassing soul alignment. The more you engage in spiritual practices such as meditation, yoga, prayer, and conscious dreaming, the better you feel, and the more you can contribute to the world and people around you.

This is also where self-love comes in. When you connect with yourself, and begin to know who you are on a deeper level, you are able to love your whole self. Your compassion, understanding, and acceptance of yourself is what ultimately opens the door of unconditional love for yourself, as well as people around you. Self-love reverberates with goodness in all directions, and shines brighter than any inner light, because it is an expression of divine love.

Meditation also helps clear our mind, and elegantly dissolves illusions. The veil between our inner and outer worlds is very thin, and the reverberations of positive or negative experiences inside the projector—that is within us—can be felt all around. In most moments of our existence, our worries are unfounded and our perceptions may even be distorted. With a dedicated meditation practice, you live from a place of higher clarity, and experience less distortion.

Meditation not only de-clutters your mind but also your home. If you love living in a clean and bright environment, and like to think of your home as organized and inviting, a daily meditation practice is a very efficient and mindful way of getting each day off to a good start. I've found that the times when my house feels messy and unorganized, are also the times in my life when I feel tired, overburdened, concerned, or emotionally weighed down. It's pretty easy to see if something is not flowing in your life. Maybe your dishes take the shape of a small mountain, letters lay around unsorted and unopened, or your house just feels heavier. Everything is connected.

Your soul's home is inside the heart of the Universe, and meditation effortlessly helps you floating back into this loving golden field—celestially connecting you with the Divine. When you connect with your soul's divine home, you flow with infinite compassion. The more mindful you become, the more your connect with this sacred inner place, and the easier it will be for you to consciously choose thoughts, feelings, and experiences that fill your heart with love and joy, and the more confidently you will rise above fears as they come along. When you keep a daily meditation practice, whether it be in a seated crossed-legged or full-lotus position, or laying on your mat in Savasana after a yoga class, you flow with love and grace, meet each day in the present moment, and vibrate in golden alignment.

Dreamy Affirmations for
MEDITATING WITH GRACE

—◦◦◦◦—

BELONG
Meditation brings me back
to where I was all along,
and eternally belong.

* * *

MEDITATION
I keep a wondrous meditation practice each day
It keeps all negative patterns away.

* * *

THE LIGHT OF MY SOUL
In the warming rays of the sun,
my home is enlightened
Everything is so bright
my senses have been heightened.
I take a step out the door
and I'm showered with light
from the sun of my soul.
Never before
have I felt this ready to soar.

* * *

INNER GRACE

I greet people with love in my heart,
I connect with a smile on my face,
because it is my inner grace,
that makes this world a loving place

* * *

LIGHT SOUL

I am a light soul,
I spin and flow above illusions.

* * *

AWAKENED STATE

For each conscious breath I take
I choose to vibrate at a higher level of existence
and lovingly experience myself in an awakened state
of mind.

* * *

THE GOLDEN FIELD

My soul's home
is in a golden field,
of divine love,
and soft stillness.

PRACTICE 11: MEDITATE WITH GRACE

(a) This is your time to experience the blissful state of pure consciousness, and float out in a field of soft stillness and infinite love. Sit comfortably with your spine straight, or if you prefer, lay down on a yoga mat. Visualize bright light entering through the top of your head, immersing your entire body with light. See how you are the light, and expand your energy in all directions.

(b) In this bright state, create an affirmation of infinite love and light.

(c) Say your affirmation out load, then close your eyes, and place your right hand on your heart. Breathe in love. Breathe out love. Stay in this loving frequency as long as you wish.

12

Pray with Your Soul

There is a golden glow
shining from deep inside the rainbow.
In this loving place so bright,
everything is set right.

DIVINE LOVE BEGINS in our heart and transcends any perceived notions of separation. Our true nature is oneness, and omnipresent love helps us reach a sacred awareness where everything is connected, and *we* are *one*. Aligning yourself with the frequency of your soul, and becoming one with what you wish and pray for—and then feeling every experience from this loving vibration, caress the material that ultimately creates the golden key to living a life in full expression. We all share an inner calling to enhance our awareness, and live with ever-flowing love in our heart. We seek higher wisdom, universal understanding, and above all we have an eternal quest for divine connection in all that we do.

The heart of the Universe vibrates with a frequency of love, compassion, and infinite wisdom. This divine frequency is your original golden state of existence. When you engage in activities that inspire you on a deep soul level, your consciousness softly expands into the frequency of your soul's home. It is in this sacred place that you remember the divine connection you have so been longing for, and it is here that you begin to dream with your soul and create with your heart. With a devoted practice of continuously remembering this golden connection—your path is brightly illuminated by your soul's light, and you lightly flow with the loving energies of the Universe. This is where you remember your highest purpose, and begin to dream with your soul and live with your heart.

Around the same time that I had my profound dream of the power of believing in what I can do, I had another dream that ended up impacting me just as deeply. In the dream I feared that I would lose someone near and dear to me, and I began praying with all my heart that this person wouldn't die. In that very moment, I heard a voice in the dream:

> Pray for what you wish to happen,
> Never for what you don't wish to happen.

I was beautifully told to pray for what I wish to see happening. The art of praying is asking for what we wish for, and truly believing we have received it. This sacred message can also be found in the Bible: *"Therefore I tell you, whatever you ask in prayer, believe that you have received it, and it will be yours.* [The Bible, ESV: Mark 11.24][23]

WITH GOD ALL THINGS ARE POSSIBLE

There is something very powerful about coming together in a group, worshipping and sharing our divine love together. I have a deep love for spirituality, and feel at home wherever I feel connected to God, the Divine, the Universe—especially amongst people who love this experience just as much as I do, whether it may be a Christian church, a multi-faith spiritual center, a Buddhist temple, or a Hindu meditation garden.

Our prayers are most powerful when done from our soul's home. It is in this sacred place that you can wholly experience the fullness of the divine connection. Divine connection always begins in the heart, because your heart is the portal to your soul. When you pray in divine alignment, anything is possible. This sacred truth is also found in the Bible: "*With God all things are possible.*" [The Bible, ESV: Matthew 19.26][24]

By praying for what you wish for, from the sacred frequency of your soul's home, you shift into a higher state of consciousness, and transcend into the realm of soul dreaming. When you connect with your soul's home in the infinite golden field of divine consciousness, you remember your highest purpose and consciously choose loving experiences that enhance this connection. You make time for projects that inspire you. Best of all, you not only enrich your own soul dream, but you also sprinkle pixie dust on every soul you meet, every step of the way.

The dream of your soul manifests in your heart when you remember your divine soul alignment. You intuitively know the best answer when it's time to make choices and decisions in life, because when you live in divine alignment with your soul, you live in timeless awareness. You are backed by the celestial powers of the Universe, and it becomes clear how you are not expected to do everything yourself. The weight you previously placed on your own shoulders is lifted, and you rise beyond illusionary constraints and limitations. When you live in soul alignment, you have the whole Universe behind you, and the Universe helps you fulfill the dream of your soul.

Always stay true to being you. Whatever you feel called to do—may it be serving small children, protecting the environment, meditating in a monastery, singing in a choir, writing in the early morning hours, or leading a country—be sure to remember your highest purpose. Living in soul alignment is your supreme assignment.

Pray with Your Soul

When you remember your soul connection, you live in love and your heart opens like a lotus flower. Your life unfolds like a dream. In the sacred place of divine soul alignment, your consciousness expands like the sun, and the whole Universe unites as one.

Dreamy Affirmations for
PRAYING WITH YOUR SOUL

—◦◦◦◦—

THE ETERNAL PRAYER

All-encompassing divine,
Please help me stay eternally aligned,
connected, peaceful, and kind.

* * *

ETERNALLY ALIGNED

Embraced by true love divine,
I float in peace of mind,
I have awakened to my purpose,
I am eternally aligned.

* * *

LOVED AND SAFE

I am loved and protected.

* * *

WHAT I AM

What I feel I am
What I believe I am
What I see I am
What I am, I am

* * *

MANY ROADS TO FAIRYLAND

There are many roads to fairyland
There is always one close at hand
My inner magic leads the way
Whenever I close my eyes and pray.

* * *

MIRACLE OF DIVINE ALIGNMENT

The miracle of divine alignment is experienced
when I live, love, give, serve, and receive in a state
of love and gratitude.

PRACTICE 12: PRAY WITH YOUR SOUL

(a) Read the affirmations above, and feel the divine connection in your heart.
(b) From this sacred place, practice praying for what you wish to happen, and only for what you wish to happen.
(c) If you find yourself wishing for something not to happen, acknowledge the thought, and express gratitude for having the awareness to correct it.

Dreamy Affirmations for Dreaming & Believing

WHEN YOU LIVE in alignment with your soul's home you experience the magnificence of wholeness. This is where you fulfill the dream of your soul.

1. My consciousness is aligned with my soul's frequency.
2. I tune into the frequency of how I'd like to feel.
3. My heart is the portal to my soul.
4. I make wishes with all my heart.
5. I am grateful and my heart is open.
6. My heart is open and it vibrates in perfect resonance with my soul.
7. I live in a state of wonder and gratitude and welcome miracles as they flow into my life.
8. Meditation helps me expand into the golden field of my soul's home.
9. I live with clear intentions, and the Universe opens new doors for me.
10. I believe in dreams that grow in my heart.

11. I keep my inspiration flowing by looking at my life as a big university.
12. I am up early every morning, and I make the morning mine.
13. Setbacks help me develop more clarity about what it is I really want.
14. I understand, accept, and love myself with reverence. Self-love leads to loving compassion for all of humanity.
15. I pray for what I wish to happen.
16. Every dream illuminates my life.
17. I practice yoga, mindfulness, and meditation every day, and bring this higher awareness with me into my dreams.
18. I ask my dreams for guidance.
19. I am of service to people around me, and connect with all living beings with an open heart.
20. In my dreams I am not confined by time and space. There are infinite opportunities to explore possibilities.
21. I expand into the golden field of my soul's home each day, and live with an open heart.
22. The Universe helps me fulfill the dream of my soul when I live in soul alignment.
23. When I remember my soul connection my life unfolds like a dream.
24. Living in soul alignment is my supreme assignment.

Dreamy Ruminations

HYMN TO THE LAND DOWN UNDER

Born on top of the world
with a quest to go down under
she followed her dreams
and explored the land of wonder
She listened to the land
and heard stories she could understand
She had found herself anew
In a place where dreams come true.

* * *

I AM WHAT I WANT

With an inviting smile
she turns to me and says,
"The answer is within you.
The Universe does not respond to what you want
it responds to what you are."
She embraces me, and whispers,
"Are you that, what you want?"

* * *

THE CALYPSO GIRL

By the turquoise ocean,
with lips touched by sea salt,
her skin has a golden glow
as she dances on the sand,
to the sound of calypso.

* * *

THE CORAL GIRL

On a little island built on corals,
the girl walks softly on the sand
Moving gently,
she breathes in the sweet blend of sea salt and floral.
Sun-kissed with a golden tan,
she gives me a radiant smile,
and waves her hand.

* * *

DREAMS AHOY

I swim in the ocean
I dance in the moonlight
I let my dreams set sail.

* * *

DRAGONFLY

Enticing little dragonfly,
your essence is enthralling
when I see you in the sky
I know adventure is calling.

* * *

KARMA MANTRA

Two monks dressed in golden robes, turn their heads
up and smile knowingly as they say,
"It's the little things in life, all your small reactions –
that create your Karma.
I sigh and wonder what has brought on this drama,
and what I can do to clear my karma.
The monks keep smiling, gently blending flowers and
herbs in a lustrous bowl.
"Sing a mantra," they say.
"I already know some," I say. I bow to show my
gratitude, and sing with my heart.

* * *

THE CAVE OF DREAMS

Majestic dream guides in faraway land,
I come with a wish I hope you'll understand,
I once heard of the Cave of Dreams,
where time stands still, or never were

I wish to tell the story,
of the cave in its glory,
I know I have the quest,
to the angels and dream guides I leave the rest
Please help me find the way,
I want to hear the stories that were once told,
The legend says, each time a dreamer entered this
magical place,
a fairy blowed a grande horn,
This way, everyone knew a new story was
about to be born
Divine dream guides of the cave,
I think a new story is formed
I just heard the big horn!

* * *

THE FOREST MAN
In the deep majestic woods,
his heart was touched by a nightingale's soft interlude,
a forest man at heart,
he found comfort in solitude
among bullfinches, moose and cuckoos

* * *

THE LITTLE AIRPLANE

Go little airplane,
spread your wings
see the world,
from way up high,
fly with the birds,
come hear them sing

* * *

MONSTERS IN THE NIGHT

Monsters and dangerous animals
sometimes come in the night
but trust me when I say,
it will all be all right.
Just reach out your arm,
wave and smile with all your charm
and pray from your heart
your light will help them depart

* * *

BABY COCO

Everyone is going away,
and Coco is lonely in the day,
but in the evening everything is ok,
now everyone is here to stay.
It's time to snuggle up and end the day

* * *

THE DREAMERS

When the darkness of fear is near,
and all you can feel is confusion and fear,
maybe some days even wishing you could disappear,
I beg of you, dreamers,
please remember the light in your heart,
because it is your eternal brightness
that will set this world apart.
Your inner candle of love and hope will guide the
believers
You are the dreamers,
please connect with your light, and help awaken this
world,
and let your inner candle lead us as we awaken to a
more loving place.
Peace eternal rests in your love and grace.

* * *

THE FOREST FAIRY

There's a forest fairy so cute,
with wings so light and bright,
She loves playing her flute,
in the early moonlight

* * *

CHOOSE LOVE

When you find yourself at a crossroads,
faced with life decisions,
always choose to the best of your ability,
But never despair,
Because life is a spectrum of two possibilities.
No matter how much you prepare,
Life can take you anywhere,
On one side is Love,
On the other is Fear.
They live on each side of the spear.
If you ever find yourself in Fear,
Choose Love, and you will soon be there.

FAIRYLAND

The land of the fairies is an enchanting place.
The houses are made of clay,
everything is tiny and quaint,
and the air is softly sprinkled with
strawberry seeds and orange blossoms,

If you ever feel lost, dream of this magical realm,
listen closely to the music in the wind,
the song of the fairies will bring you here,

ENCHATNING WORDS

Bliss	Freedom	Opulent
Believe	Frequency	Oracle
Captivate	Generous	Palace
Charisma	Glimmer	Passion
Charming	Grace	Paradise
Cliffs	Gratitude	Pixie dust
Compassion	Glow	Prophet
Creativity	Happiness	Queen
Dance	Heaven	Radiant
Delightful	Hope	Rainbow
Discovery	Idyllic	Rich
Divine	Illumination	Romance
Dolphin	Illusion	Sage
Dragon	Imagination	Serene
Dream	Impeccable	Shaman
Elephant	Infinite	Shimmer
Elf	Inspiration	Solitude
Embrace	Joy	Sparkle
Effervescent	Kind	Spirit
Eloquence	Kingdom	Tranquility
Enchanted	Legend	Troll
Encourage	Love	Unicorn
Enlighten	Luxurious	Vision
Esoteric	Magical	Warm
Eternal	Magnificent	Wealth
Evanescent	Memorable	Whisper
Extraordinary	Mermaid	Wisdom
Fairy	Miracles	Wonder

Notes

1. Neville, G. *The Power of Awareness,* Camarillo, CA: DeVorss Publications, 2005
2. Dyer, W.W. *The Power of Intention*: *learning to co-create your world your way*, Carlsbad, CA: Hay House Inc., 2004
3. Clason, S. George. *The Richest Man in Babylon, 2014 edition.* New York, NY: Penguin Putnam Inc
4. ESV Bible: Mark 9.23 (The Holy Bible, English Standard Version ®, copyright © 2001 by Crossway, a publishing ministry of Good News Publishers. Used by permission. All rights reserved."
5. Björklund, AK. (2012). *Dream Guidance: Interpret Your Dreams and Create the Life You Desire.* Newport Beach, CA: Crystal Souls.
6. Todeschi, K.J. (1998) *Edgar Cayce on the Akashic Records.* Virginia Beach, VA: Edgar Cayce Foundation
7. Rinpoche, T.W. *The Tibetan Yogas of Dream and Sleep,* Ithaca, NY: Snow Lion, 1998
8. Tonkinson, R. (2003). Ambryse Dreams and the Mardu Dreaming. *Dream Travelers: Sleep*

Experiences and Culture in the Western Pacific. New York: NJ, Palgrave Macmillan

9. Hume, L. (2004). Accessing the Eternal: Dreaming "The Dreaming" and Ceremonial Performance. *Zygon: Journal of Religion & Science, 39*(1), 237-258.

10. Jung, C.G. (1963). *Memories, Dreams, Reflections*. New York, NY: Random House.

11. Mallet, R. (2006). *Time Travler: A Scientists's Personal Mission to Make Time Travel a Reality*. New York, NY: Thunder's Mouth Press.

12. Tegbrand, M. (2015). *Our Mathematical Universe: My Quest for the Ultimate Nature of Reality.* New York, NY: Vintage

13. Dispenza, J. (2012). *Breaking the Habit of Being Yourself: How to Lose Your Mind and Create a New one*. Carlsbad, CA: Hayhouse.

14. Cowan, J. (1992) *The Mysteries of the Dream-Time: The Spiritual Life of Australian Aborigines*. Santa Rosa, CA: Atrium Publishers Group

15. Hume, L. (2004). Accessing the Eternal: Dreaming "The Dreaming" and Ceremonial Performance. *Zygon: Journal of Religion & Science, 39*(1), 237-258.

16. Von Franz, M.L (1988) *Psyche and Matter*. Boston, MA: Shambhala Publications.

17. Moss, R. (2005). *Dreamways of the Iroquois: Honoring the Secret Wishes of the Soul*. Rochester, VT: Destiny Books.

18. Björklund, A.K. (2017). The Dream Alchemist: *A Woman's Search for Love, Bliss, and Freedom across India, Time, and Dreams*. Boiling Springs, PA: Ars Metaphysica.

19. Mandela, N. R. (1995). *A Long Walk to Freedom*. Boston, MA: Back Bay Books

20. Von Franz, M.L. (1997). *Alchemical Active Imagination*. Boston, MA: Penguin Random House.

21. Wong, E. (2011). *Taoism: An Essential Guide*. Boulder, CO: Shambala.

22. Björklund, A.K. (2017). The Dream Alchemist: *A Woman's Search for Love, Bliss, and Freedom across India, Time, and Dreams*. Boiling Springs, PA: Ars Metaphysica.

23. ESV Bible: Mark 11.24 (The Holy Bible, English Standard Version ®, copyright © 2001 by Crossway, a publishing ministry of Good News Publishers. Used by permission. All rights reserved."

24. ESV Bible: Matthew 19.26 (The Holy Bible, English Standard Version ®, copyright © 2001 by Crossway, a publishing ministry of Good News Publishers. Used by permission. All rights reserved."

About the Author

Anna-Karin Björklund M.A. is an inspirational writer and the author of *The Dream Alchemist* and *Dream Guidance*. She is also a teacher of dreams, soul growth, and yoga, and her work has been featured on Steve Harvey, Fox & Friends, and Face the Truth; in *Women's Running Magazine*, *Yours*, *Orange Coast*, *Marie Claire*, *Money*, *Mind Body Green*, and *goop*.

Anna-Karin is the Chair of the Board of the non-profit organization *The International Association for the Study of Dreams*, and is also a specialist with *Miraval Life in Balance Spa*. She holds a master's degree in counseling psychology from Argosy University in Orange, CA, and a bachelor's degree in tourism management, from University of Technology Sydney, Australia.

A passionate world explorer, she is originally from Sweden, and has lived in five countries. Her home is now in California, where she lives with her daughter and baby Coco—their bi-lingual French Bulldog. She is often found reading a good book in her little herb garden, sipping lavender tea.

www.AnnaKarinBjorklund.com